DRIV

Stephen

Sound

for Dad

DRIVING © **1987,** Stephen Barnes

Canadian Cataloguing in Publication Data

Barnes, Stephen, 1959 —
Driving

ISBN 0–920151–09–4

1. Automobile driving – Anecdotes, facetiae, satire, etc. I. Title

TL152.5.B37   1987   388.3'21'0207   C87–093644–1

Published and Printed in Canada by

**Sound And Vision Publishing Limited
84 Bleecker Street
Toronto   M4X 1L8**

1 2 3 4 5 6 7 8 9   87   90   89   88

THE AUTOMOBILE

Picture if you will, coming back to your cave from a dinosaur hunt. You've been out for days, crossing rivers, scouring jungles, being chased by prehistoric monsters. You only want to put your feet up. Then your mate reminds you of the big party tonight and says there's no mix. The corner store is two forests, three swamps and one tyrannosaurus away. It you had a car, it would be a snap. However, the wheel won't be invented for thousands of years yet. What to do?

Sure, it may cost too much to run, or never stay as clean as we'd like it to, but the automobile is our ticket out of the Stone Age. Give a caveman flush toilets, or no-stick cookware, and he's still a caveman. Give him a car, and he becomes a Driver; an independent, free-wheeling horizon-chaser! The automobile opens up new doors for his self-expression!

Stick him in a traffic jam and he becomes a caveman again.

Well, nothing's perfect . . .

A

Accident
– too depressing to start a book with . . . (*see* **Collision**)

Advertisement
– take a multi-million dollar budget, add a dash of splashy graphics, throw in a load of technical buzzwords, stir in some subliminal sex and *Presto*! the car ad is born. As a driver, you'll know you've been conned by one of these when you've just bought a car that you don't like, at a time you're not expecting, at a price you can't afford.

Aerodynamic Drag
– the resistance of air to a moving vehicle. Cars today are extremely slippery when compared to those of the '50's, when all the popular ones had massive fenders and tail fins that created a huge drag. Many drivers, however, considered this to be less of a drag than not owning a car with massive fenders and tail fins.

Airbag
– government legislator pushing for passive restraint systems in vehicles.

Alert
– being observant and quick to respond behind the wheel. Take care to not confuse being alert with

being a lert. Lerts are drivers who tend to over-react. For example, on an icy hill an alert driver would shift into low gear for a gentle descent, whereas a lert would lock the brakes in a panic and slide into statistics.

Alteration
– any modification of a vehicle from its original condition. An all-too-common one with adolescent males involves tampering with their car's muffler system, to produce a window-rattling roar.

Altercation
– heated tussle between one or more homeowners and the neighborhood adolescent male.

Amber
– traffic light quickly sandwiched between the green and red lights, notorious for its keen laxative effect on drivers rapidly approaching intersections.

Animal

– any creature content with bad breath - a fine example being the dog. Experts have suggested that the brightness and shape of certain cars excites the primal hunting instincts in dogs. This means a hound chasing your car is mistaking it for a giant squirrel, which can be very embarrassing, both for you and the dog. Most drivers find that steadily accelerating away can alleviate this canine nuisance. Problems arise, however, when Fido can outrun your car. In this case it's wise to:

1/ consider selling your car.

2/ try driving away in reverse. It'll confuse the dog, and should give you good practice at backing up.

We've all had close calls with hitting animals while driving. Sure, it's hard to get worked up over bugs splattering on the windshield . . . we can't hear their last-minute screams, and a flick of the washer/wiper can erase the goo in a jiffy. And, while rabbits and turtles are enough trouble themselves, it's the really big game that matters. Consider, for instance, bagging a moose at 100 km/hr. Talk about forcing a change of plans in your day. Not to mention the moose's day. Remember to slow down when you see moose and deer crossing signs. When one does leap across your path, it won't look like it does in the picture:

No, it'll be more like:

Apex

– 1/ innermost point of a corner on a race track.

2/ outermost pedestrian on a corner at an intersection.

Artery

– radio traffic reporters' term for a major metropolitan roadway.

Artichoke

– expression frequently used by radio traffic reporters during rush hours.

Automatic

– 1/ (*fam.*) hydrodynamic coupling device used to propel a vehicle by mating its engine to the driveshaft.

2/ the relationship between being late for work, and having every traffic light on the way turn red.

B

Backfire

– attempting repairs at home to save money, and having their corrections at a garage cost more than the original work would have.

Back Seat Driver
– only removable accessory to come with keen insights, quick reflexes and 360° vision.

Bank Manager
– *see* **Villain.**

Bicyclist
– moving obstacle. Sharing the road with motorists as they do could qualify most cyclists as "drivers", though the added dimension of hazard to being on a 10 kg. two-wheeler threading between potholes, fenders and sewer grates brings other names to mind - like Loon and Cabbagehead.

Given the rivalry for road space between motorists and cyclists, tensions could be eased with a few considerations:

Bikers: For Pete's sake obey the rules of the road if you want respect. Whizzing past stop signs without even looking guilty is no way to do it.

Motorists: Don't lose patience, and don't try to hang a right immediately in front of the cyclist you just flew past - the body tumbling over your hood may be the one you just cut off.

Survival of the Fittest Dep't.

If you're being chased by a dog (*see* **Animal**), above all STAY COOL. There's nothing more annoying than riding into the back of a parked car while keeping an eye on the fangs at your feet. Sometimes, slowing down actually works, as many dogs turn into chickens if you call their bluff. Should this fail, (signalled by the dog trying to tackle your bike) there are still a few options open to you:

1/ Perhaps the one chasing you is simply in heat, and wants to mate with your shoe. Carry a water bottle to spray these types of sick-o's.

2/ If things look serious, try throwing scraps of raw meat. Expensive - yes, but look at it as a toll fee. And forget trying to cut costs by substituting other foods . . . don't risk your legs by tossing bits of tofu to some beast that can run faster than you can peddle.

Bicyclist

T-BONE-FREE

CARDBOARD TRAFFIC
INTIMIDATOR

* good visibility
* bolts on
  in
  minutes!

* lightweight

Cyclist in
van driver
position

* fun on
  windy
  days!

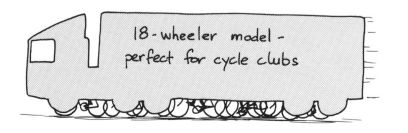

18-wheeler model –
perfect for cycle clubs

sufficient
ground clearance
for most
turns

Billboards

– hardy, roadside members of the fungus family which grow several metres high . . . particularly 5 miles, 4 miles, 3 miles, 2 miles, 1 mile, and ½ mile ahead of many highway diners in the U.S.A.

Blind Spot

– area extending from a driver's field of vision, in which nothing is apparent.

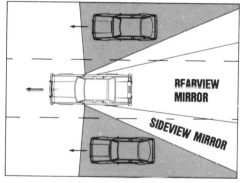

COMMON BLIND SPOTS

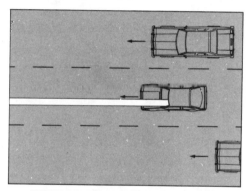

MONDAY MORNING BLIND SPOT

Blowout

– 1/ uncommon but dangerously rapid loss of air from a tire.

   2/ very common and rapid loss of gunk and carbon deposits from the engine when a car is driven with great *elan*.

Boost

- lift in your spirits felt when someone pulls up to your dead car with jumper cables.

Booze

- (*slang*) alcoholic beverage. If cars had the good sense of motorcycles, they would fall over in parking lots on drivers who've had too much to drink.

Bore

- 1/ engine cylinder diameter.
  2/ hot rodder talking about 1/.

Brakes

- 1/ "Those are the brakes". Commonly said by mechanics to their customers when looking under the car.
  2/ "Those are the breaks". Commonly said by mechanics to their customers when looking at the repair bill.

Braking

- the art of slowing down or stopping a vehicle, either by using the brakes, or downshifting.

Broken

- condition of anything in the vicinity of a driver not braking properly.

Buckle Up
- what safety-conscious drivers do with seat belts, and what springtime thaws do with pavement.

Bumper
- 1/ tactile parking gauge.
2/ person who never really "totals" a car but instead accumulates dents.

Burning Rubber
- accelerating madly to cause the drive wheels to spin in place - which makes the tires overheat - thus creating a "smoke show". Goes hand-in-hand with burning money.

C

California
- Mecca of automobile *aficionados*. More Lamborghinis, Maseratis, Ferraris, Jacuzzis and loonis are to be found here than anywhere else in the world.

Carsick
- becoming ill when travelling in a vehicle - the symptoms being dizziness, cramps and nausea. Usually this is no cause for alarm, though drivers should be examined if they cough up fur balls during a full moon.

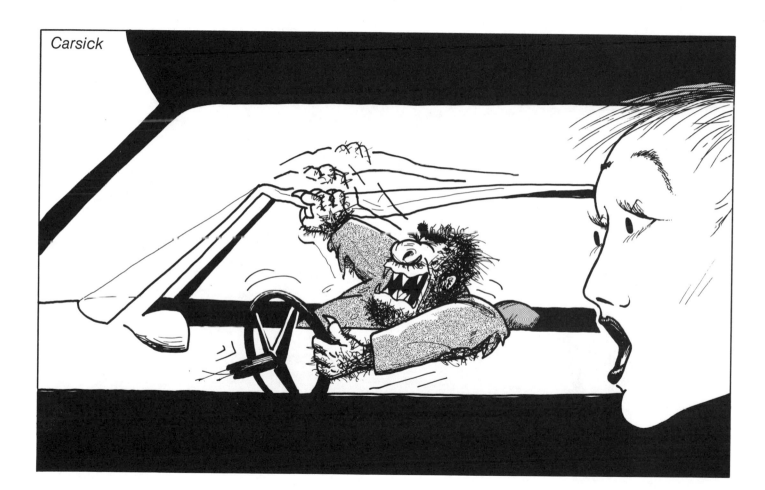

Choke

- 1/ butterfly valve in carburetor that would - if it worked properly - ease cold-weather starting.
  2/ irrational, physical response, aimed at anything in reach of a driver whose car won't start.

Citizen Band

– Russian pop group of the '70's that gained underground success with such hits as "How Much is That Auto in the Window?" and "Some Day My Car Will Come". When discovered by Politburo chiefs, the group was disbanded and members were assigned to several years hard labour in a tire-retreading plant near Minsk.

Clutch

– 1/ mechanical or hydraulic friction device used to stall the engine when starting on hills.
2/ what passengers then do to their seats.

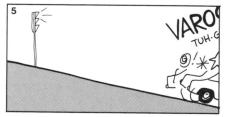
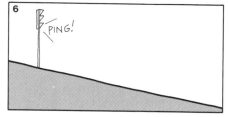

Collision

– blight on transportation since the dawn of history. This Mesopotamian wall fresco, c. 3200 B.C., depicts the first recorded collision. Notice the similarities to accidents nowadays, excepting of course the carriages and mens' skirts.

Comatose

– condition of most drivers jamming the centre lanes of a highway.

Computers

– electronic information devices that are not as new to driving as we may think. Long ago, the Popular Handyman magazine predicted that by 1965 we'd all be driving cars controlled by computers. This lofty hope was a tad premature, for when they sponsored a contest to design computer-guided cars, the results were disastrous. Numerous vehicles became lost, and several entries mistook driveways for sidestreets, and turned into them - wiping out garages at over 60 km/hr. In a fit of what can only be described as mass suicide, none of the remaining vehicles remembered to roll up its windows for the Car Wash Test.

 P.H. magazine scrapped this effort as "too ambitious", though there is talk they expect within 30 years Man will jog to the moon with computerized rocket shoes. Test volunteers remain scarce . . .

Cruising

– curious social ritual aimed at impressing members of the opposite sex. Though not exclusively so, it is typically practised by the male of the species. Some examples and their respective success rates with the females are:

ANIMAL	TECHNIQUE USED	SUCCESS RATE
Peacock (bird)	Parades in front of female. Punctuates this with explosive fanning of colourful tail. Makes sound like: "Arrrrahh Ka.!"	95%
Himey Egrec (lizard)	Rears up on hind legs, dances by female swinging arms haughtily while turning green all over.	nearly 100%
Man (homosapien)	Drives past women in car with windows down and stereo blaring. Repeats this *ad nauseam* by circling the block. Caps off effort with remarks like "whoop whoop whoop" and, when desperate, revs engine and screeches tires.	trace

Curb

– stationary whitewall remover.

D

Defrost
- powerful hot air setting in car, capable of melting ice caked on the windshield.

Defrostee
- any occupant of a vehicle who suffers acute hypothermia while waiting for the defroster to warm up.

Demerit Points
- civilized method of penalizing bad drivers. Sharply contrasts the less effective, earlier police tricks like crude facial gestures, and taunts like, "Are those ears on your head, or did you just open your doors?"

Detours
- on debusses can be great for depeople who hate dedriving.

Dotted Line
- pavement marking that permits the passing of slower vehicles. Regrettably, this only appears at the same locations as oncoming traffic.

Drivers (the Bus Driver)

Downshift
– direction taken in financial status when insurance premiums are paid.

Drive-In
– revolutionary concept in Western consumerism whereby drivers can receive goods and services while remaining in their vehicles. Growing numbers of psychologists claim this obsessive attachment to the automobile stems from early childhood. According to one doctor, "Infants in strollers are in fact hoaxes - merely faking spasticness in order to get a free ride from life, as if not having any teeth somehow justifies being wheeled around all day! They get spoiled by this spongey-bottomed lifestyle of theirs, and BINGO! they're hooked . . . a lifelong dependency on the car . . . "

Drivers
– 1/ **the Beginner** - typically found doing unorthodox things: adhering religiously to speed limits, taking traffic signs seriously, and yielding to other drivers. Often spotted backing into the garden beside the driveway.

– 2/ **the Bus Driver** - rumour has it that many bus drivers are raised in the wild by gorillas. It's easy to see the connection . . . in the tiny country of Yam, trained gorillas have been driving buses for years. Although broken of their habitual panic-braking tendencies, these primates still insist on taking corners at 60 km/hr. and accelerating away before elderly people are seated. Research continues . . .

– 3/ **the Hero** - takes it upon himself (Heroes being typically male) to rescue the streets from the ravages of his noisy, fire-breathing monster (any model of car will do). Quite distinguished for his uncanny knack of avoiding many accidents in spite of a shortage of both competence and common sense. Found in great abundance on two-wheeled crotch rockets (*see* **Motorcycle**).

– 4/ **the Houseparent** - never gets out much. Typified by an almost overcautious technique behind the wheel. Heaven forbid if highway driving should be necessary. Only uses mirrors for emergencies - like backing up and checking hair.

– 5/ **the Regular Joe/Jane** - these people make up your basic "cast of thousands" on the roads. Most are indifferent towards driving - only wanting to get from point A to point B without an accident or high costs. If a twisty road comes up, they're capable of enjoying sporty driving, though pleasure will drop off sharply if they know the car needs a wash.

– 6/ **the Senior Citizen** - comes in two types:
   a) oblivious to all speed limits, traffic signs, and other drivers
   b) *see* **the Beginner**.

– 7/ **the Taxi Driver** - professional Hero. Often the most impatient to get started at a green light and least likely to stop for an amber one. Pedestrians take note: think of the crosswalk not as your right-of-way, so much as no-man's land. Remember, the cabbie tearing towards you may be seeing you as a target if you're not hailing him. If so, your best defense is to carry several large suitcases and look lost. This way you're sure to look like a potential fare - the last person a cabbie would run over.

– 8/ **the Sunday Driver** - frequently spotted treating green-light intersections as 4-way stops. This street snail holds the perverse view of driving as something akin to wine tasting . . . it can only be enjoyed when savoured slowly. Frustrating to follow, especially on hilly, winding, 2-lane roads when you've got a bladder-full of deadlines.

– 9/ **the Woman Driver** - inept, uptight, woodenheaded, careless female who has no right to be on the road. Most harshly criticized by inept, uptight, woodenheaded, careless males who have no right to be on the road.

Driving Abroad
- unflattering taxi driver slang referring to female fares.

Driving Examiner
- omnipotent, sadistic biped who can make even the most lion-hearted soul tremble with fear. Typical government employee.

Education
- something most drivers don't think they need. Perhaps it's time for a driving manual that better reflects what street-wise drivers come to learn after years on the road. The examples may be something like:

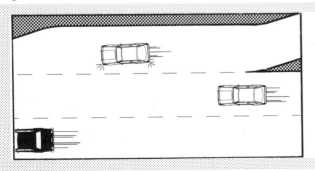

IN MERGING ONTO THE HIGHWAY, YOU SHOULD:
- **a**) accelerate gently into the right–hand lane
- **b**) sound horn and dive for the left–hand lane.
- **c**) come to a full stop until you can't see anything coming.

b) Although **a** & **c** are popular, **b** is most correct. Think of driving as a tennis game, with merging as the serve. It's your chance to assert your aggression, and take control of what follows.

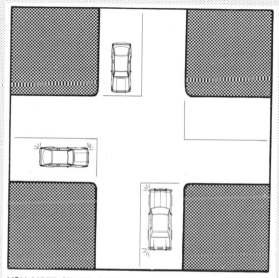

YOU MEET OTHER CARS AT A 4-WAY STOP. THE
RIGHT-OF-WAY SHOULD GO TO THE DRIVER WHO IS:

   a) on the right.
   b) sounding horn.
   c) in the most expensive car.

c) The most expensive car. Keep in mind this person
may be able to afford a better lawyer than you if there's
an accident.

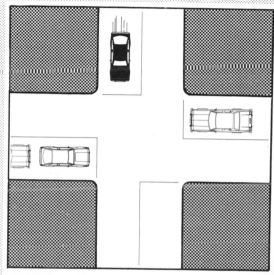

YOU'RE APPROACHING AN INTERSECTION AND THE
LIGHT TURNS AMBER. YOU SHOULD:

   a) gently come to a stop.
   b) proceed with caution.
   c) sound horn and accelerate.

c) Sound horn and accelerate. Check behind you . . .
several cars are likely doing the same thing.

YOU'VE JUST BACKED OVER YOUR NEIGHBOR AND HER DOG. YOU SHOULD:

a) sound horn and try again.

b) drive away and hope they'll be gone when you return.

c) give them immediate aid and report the incident to the authorities at once.

c) While **a & b** are likely tempting, the most responsible choice would be **c**. When choosing an authority to contact, most people select the police out of habit. You may want to try your local golf pro, or some university professors – authorities far less likely to give you legal hassles than the police.

Emergencies

– Big problems. For instance: a Neanderthal man on a motorcycle cuts in front of you. You blast him with your horn, and wave your fist threateningly. As you pull up to the next stop light, he's there with buddies. You're in a convertible. Big help your CAA membership is now.

England

- only country in which stuffing one's bonnet into another's boot can result in whiplash.

Quickie Primer of English Terms

England	North America
lyre	*tire*
lorry	*truck*
saloon	*sedan*
pub	*saloon*
gearchange	*1) gearshift*
	2) rearrangement of luggage
dynamo	*1) generator*
	2) spry member of opposite sex
petrol	*gas*
gas	*fart*
wrong side of the road	*right side of the road*

Motoring through the English countryside can turn up countless cheery inns. Deciding on which one to stop at can simplified by consulting a tour book, such as "The Queen's Guide to Inns and Pub Food". This review of Royal Family roadside haunts lists their favourite stops to wolf down steak and kidney pies and quaff some pints. Among the inns receiving 4-crown ratings were: The Pig & Whistle, The Duck & Thistle, The Rain & Dristle, The Bomb & Mistle, and The Steak & Gristle.

Etiquette
– involves stifling your urge to dart into a small opening in traffic, then waiting an eternity for another chance.

Fast
– thrilling rate of speed. Name given to car capable of such.

Fasting
– not eating in order to save money for a fast car.

Fire Hydrants
– car repellants beamed from U.F.O.'s into every available parking spot in a city.

Fishtail
– descriptive term coined for the serpentine path a car follows during certain skids. An extremely rapid fishtail could be called a *Puppydogtail*, while a married woman in this situation is experiencing a *Wivestail*, and overeaters would have a *Pigstail* on their hands.

Countless people have wet themselves in anxiety when they've begun skidding, not realizing that

with a cool head and some deft coordination they could wipe out their problem instead of a lamppost. In light of the fact that most people do the opposite of what's required in a panic situation, the following are appropriate measures to take when skidding to the outside of a highway curve:

1/ Scream
2/ Cover eyes with hands
3/ Slam on brakes
4/ Scream
5/ Duck below dashboard
6/ Scream

Flares
– soggy red things that are crushed flat under junk in the trunk. The only security flares can provide in a nighttime emergency will be from the glow of the matches that you try to light them with.

Flat
– name and shape of a tire which has lost its air. Having flats is known as the "pits". Found regularly in the pits was famed Indianapolis racer of the '30's, "Flats" Hannigan. He holds the record for the most punctures suffered (17) in one race. His cold rivalry with fellow competitor "Tacks" Avery has been cause for speculation.

Flat-Out
– 1/ driving a car at its limits of control, which are often above those of the driver.
2/ prone position of most things after being struck by a car being driven flat-out.

Changing A Flat In The Dark

1   Find trunk keyhole.

2   Open trunk, and begin removing power tools, jugs of anti-freeze, baseball equipment, moldly news-paper, kids' toys, and oil cans.

3   Poke around further to locate the jack, the lug-wrench (usually sharp-edged steel items) and the spare tire.

4   Assemble jack. Then take it apart and re-assemble it correctly. Then take it apart again and re-assemble it even more correctly.

5   Don't look directly into the head-lights of approaching cars.

6   Select a level, solid point from which to jack up the car. (Best done by groping around on hands and knees.)

7 After raising the car, pop off the hubcap, realize you need to loosen the lug nuts with the car on the ground or the wheel'll spin, lower the car, loosen the nuts, raise the car, remove the nuts, place them in the hubcap for safe keeping, and set it aside.

8 Exchange the spare with the flat. Begin feeling around for the hubcap with the lug nuts.

9 Keep feeling.

10 Once found, replace the cursed nuts on the wheel, lower the car, tighten the nuts, and begin trying to remount the hubcap.

11 Who cares about the #@**! hubcap at this hour? Give up on it. Toss the jack, lug-wrench, and hubcap in the trunk, and get back on the road.

12 Turn around after 10 minutes, when you remember you didn't repack the power tools, jugs of anti-freeze, baseball equipment, moldly newspaper, kids' toys, oil cans, and the flat tire.

Flooding The Engine
– one of several beastly treatments of vehicles rumoured to soon be banned by law. Other offences would include: the slamming of doors, hammering the brakes, grinding the gears, smoking the tires, gunning the motor, hitting the gas, stripping the threads, and depressing the clutch.

Fog
– reliable source of solid, immovable objects.

Fuel Injection
– consolation-prize option for drivers who really wanted a turbo.

Full
– something a driver's gas tank and wallet likely aren't at the same time.

G-Force
– mysterious, almost magnetic attraction between a car on a curve, and the guardrail. Expressions like "Gee . . . !", (and others less printable) have been inspired by this.

Garage
– special room of the house used to shelter gardening equipment, kids' toys, old furniture and

Gears (Assorted Shift Patterns)

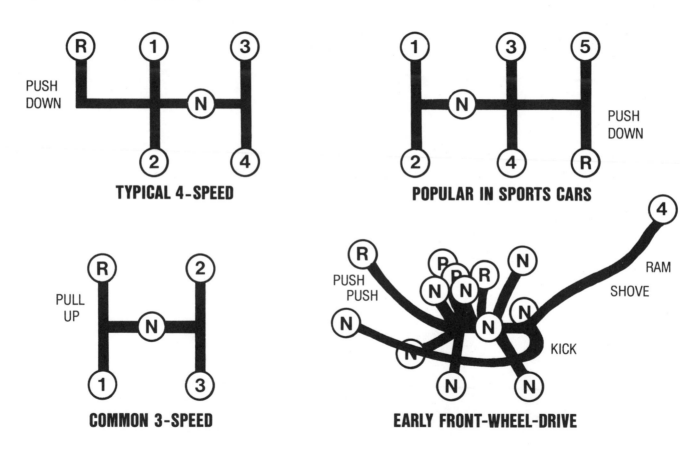

TYPICAL 4-SPEED

POPULAR IN SPORTS CARS

COMMON 3-SPEED

EARLY FRONT-WHEEL-DRIVE

garbage; outside of which the car is parked.

Gas

– what a driver gets from stopping at highway service centres, both by filling at the pumps, and eating at the restaurant.

Gears

– given regularly to their customers by some dealership parts departments. The driver walks in and says, *"Good day! I'd like a horn button for my Fettucine GT."* What the driver then gets is the 'gears' instead of the desired part:

"No can do, sir, we'll have to order it. If it's in the warehouse it could take from four weeks until oh, say, forever . and we'll need your car as a deposit."

"Gag."

The driver then gets home dejected, whereupon the spouse asks, *"Did you get your button, dear?".*

"No, they just gave me the gears."

Once the part does arrive, it has to be paid for:

"That'll be $104.60 please."

"Gag."

"Sorry, it only comes as an assembly."

On returning home, again the question, *"Did you get your button, dear?"*

"Uh-huh . . . and I got the gears again."

Glove Compartment
- dashboard space that's crammed full of maps of nowhere you want to go to (and none of where you're now headed), more than a dozen broken pencils, useless receipts, invalid coupons, sand and no gloves.

Head Restraints
- in automotive terms, simply the headrest on the seat - the development of which owes little to other head restraints such as halucinogenic drugs, tight hats, and very low doorways.

Heel and Toe
- sports car magazine of the '30's, known for its topical features, like Windshield Wipers: Are They Here To Stay?, and Lane Changes - How To Make Them Work For You.

Hidden Dangers
- unexpected perils. Caution must be taken when coming upon anything that may be blocking potential hazards from your view. Before cresting a hill for instance, you should ask yourself, "What could be on the other side? And how soft is it"?. When approaching a row of parked cars, it may be wise to wonder, "What could possibly dart out from between these cars to cause almost certain tragedy?" And if a hidden danger does take you by surprise, be prepared to make snap decisions like,

"Would it be better to veer off over that cliff, or swerve head-on into the brick wall?".

In the unlikely event these simple precautions would incite paranoia in a driver, further questioning might be called for, such as, "Why not take the train?".

Hitch-hiker

– curious growth which springs up primarily near highway on-ramps, and on nearly every street in a university town. As a driver, you should be aware of some precautions when dealing with hitch-hikers: a) never eat any food offered to you by a hiker if the hiker refuses to eat it first.

b) some shady types are so desperate for rides that they'll dress up as businessmen out of gas. A few stoop so low as to carry an empty gas can, and even stand near parked cars for added impact. Steer clear of these low-lifes.

Holidays

– *term originating from:* Holy Days
modern day consequence: Hell on Wheels

Honk

– communicative gesture instinctive to most water fowl and many motorists, particularly when travelling in tight formation.

Horsepower

– turn-of-the-century movement founded by a group of horses disgruntled with the appearance of the horseless carriage. Fears of a return to field plowing were likely behind this.

Hydroplaning
– driving over wet roadways with tires that trap the water. This offers a traction coefficient roughly on par with a huge banana peel.

Ichneumon
– weasel-like quadruped that destroys crocodiles' eggs. While this may seem irrelevant to driving at first, families on long trips will appreciate using this name in a spelling bee, which could be good for nearly half a minute of peace and quiet.

Insurance Broker
– person who leaves you with no choice but to visit your bank manager (*see* **Bank Manager**).

Intersection

– most popular setting for climaxes in television dramas. Also inspirational to the Fine Arts - who can forget Monet's brilliant painting Carrefour Avec Deux Baguettes? And then there's this timeless poem:

ODE TO A CROSSROAD

– Oh ! Cursed junction,
that strikes from grasp,
my dreams of punctuality.
I gun it –
perchance to beat a yellow,
but Lo,
the newt ahead,
plays it safe,
and comes
to a
halt.
   Howling tires of mine,
do your job,
lest we punt
the slowing dogs up front!
   Blast it! We're waiting,
smothered in others' Top 40,
waiting . . . waiting . . .
   Hark!
The Green arrives,
casting consent
on our gathering queue.

A left, need I,
signal flicking,
edging forward,
creeping,
slowly . . .
At last!
A hole in traffic Now's my chance!
Oh NO!!
Wherefrom comest anon,
this herd of pedestrian cattle?
"Right of Way!" you say?
Suffer me not!
that I should yield,
to their bovine ways.
A pox on you all
and your filthy pace!
   A swerve, and
a dodge, and
I'm free of this phlegm,
to boot it again,
in time
to make the next Red.

Anonymous

Jack

J

Jack
- 1/ rickety mechanism found scattered in pieces throughout the trunk. Used to raise the corner of a car so that it can fall when the wheel is off.
  2/ name often stitched onto the overalls of the tow-truck driver called after the jack is used.

Jaguar
- animal and car most often yielded to.

Japan
- the '60's were a rough time for the Land of the Rising Sun. Its freshly-imported cars were commiting Hari Kiri in our harsh climate, and its grade B horror movies were box-office bombs. Not being ones to fall behind the times, the Japanese since then have made great strides in upgrading quality, and reading market trends. We've now got imports that people are lining up for, and a soon-to-be-released aerobics film in 3-D, "Godzilla Has a Workout".

Joy Ride
- any trip that doesn't require gas to be purchased, repairs to be made, detours to be taken, or accidents avoided. The last known joy ride occurred in 1964, to a Mrs. Hazel Tween of Flan, Michigan.

Jump

– jumping a car is easily done if one knows how. Jumper cables are of course a requisite, as are two cars, one of which should be electrically "dead". With one jumper cable, connect the two cars' positive battery terminals, squeezing the exposed clips with your bare hands to ensure a good connection. Next, grab the second cable and - standing in a puddle of water while licking the fender - hook it to the negative terminals. Reaching this stage should give the average-sized person a jump of 4-6 metres - sufficient to clear most cars and trucks.

K

Karma

– indispensible presence. Children on long car trips are said to need a strong karma in order to weather the frustrations of confinement and boredom. If well prepared, this karma will have snacks, treats, and games close at hand, to prevent the kids from distracting the karpa from his driving.

Kerchief

– standard garb for women riding in convertibles on cool days.

Kerchief!

– standard exclamation from women riding in convertibles on cool days.

Jump (the Short Cable Solution)

Kick The Tires

- term for inspecting a car. Kicking the tires when car shopping can be next to useless, though some people insist on doing it anyway, claiming "it feels neat". Nathan Ingot, head of the American-based Consumers' Rights Or We Sue (C.R.O.W.S.) suggests a refocus in strategy: " . . . try bootin' more questionable things like fenders, mirrors, and grills - which are often flimsy plastic. Likely the salesman'll need a swift hoof as well, but avoid this if you want the best deal . . ."

Kitty Litter

- ground clay that's frequently used to: a) soak up oil puddles in garages.
b) toss under drive wheels spinning on ice.
c) extend hamburger meat at highway restaurants.

Lane

- slow moving channel of traffic that looked a lot quicker than the one you were previously in, which now looks alot quicker than the one you're presently in.

Leak

- any noise, cloud, or puddle that comes from a break, hole, or rip and leads to curses, kicks, and debts.

Learner's Permit
- certificate allowing its bearer to wreak all of the usual havoc on the roads without being licensed to do so.

Lemon
- popular addition to mixed drinks and wrecking yards.

License
- operator's permit given to qualified drivers. What exactly constitutes a qualified driver is anybody's guess, but allegations have been made that a person who can butter toast has the skills needed to ace a driving exam. In light of these criticisms, transportation officials are cracking down with tougher standards - rumoured to be on par with preparing a full-course dinner for six complete with appetizers.

Lie
- traditional used car sales pitch.

List
- crucial pre-trip plan itemizing indispensible things to be remembered.

Lost
- what lists often become at the last minute.

Lemon

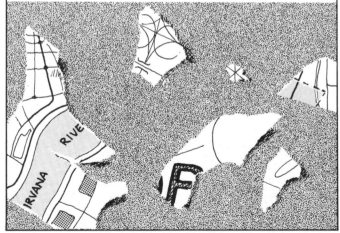

Lust
– unbridled longing for fast cars, open roads, and lost lists.

Maps
– frequent holiday travelling companions. Spelled backwards, also a frequent holiday travelling companion. Maps can be lifesavers at times, though ironically many people suffer heart attacks trying to refold them. At this year's World Map Refolding Championships, held in Athens, past champion Jean Michelin caused a stir by refolding a road map of Europe and North Africa in under 10 minutes. Michelin nearly lost his crown to Indian whiz Madan Mohan, until Mohan was disqualified for tucking Portugal under Spain by folding the creases backwards.

Merge
– little-known town in Saskatchewan settled on the island formed by an obscure road headed nowhere in particular, and the on-ramp that meets it from somewhere else.

Mistakes
– you've just made an automotive *faux pas.* How do you save your dignity?

Here are some tips:

YOU WANT TO:	INSTEAD, YOU:	NOW YOU SHOULD:
change your grip on the steering wheel	honk the horn	not pay attention to the driver in front of you, who's likely looking around in anger - rather, pretend you've spotted someone on the sidewalk, and wave. Don't be distracted by people waving back, though; you may have an accident . . . with the driver in front of you.
push the cassette eject button on your radio	push the cigarette lighter	let the lighter pop out. If you smoke, light up a cigarette. If not, then tell your passengers, ''. . . fixed it yesterday, just testing...'', and toss it back in with disgust as if it still needs work. THEN flip the cassette.
park your car	back into a drainage ditch	climb from the car as if you always park it like this. If asked about the 45° angle the car is on, ''it's for the oil level . . . '' should stifle further questions.

Money
– endangered species rarely seen in large numbers by most drivers.

Motorcycle
– motor-driven two-wheeled vehicle that falls over easily, usually to the side least scratched and dented from previous falls. The trick to avoiding this embarrassment is to ensure that the bike matches the biker, which is best done by comparing their heights, weights, and I.Q.'s. Some types of motorcycles on the market today are:

a) the Chopper- typically very shiny, and awkward to sit on. Great for showing pride of ownership and toughness of buttock.

b) the Crotch Rocket- capable of incredible acceleration and high speeds. For those riders who laugh at danger, spit in the eye of risk, and refuse to close covers before striking.

c) the Land Yacht- "fully dressed" touring bike that can travel any distance at any speed. When purchasing these pricey cycles, riders often look for options like pneumatic suspension adjusters, hydraulic valve adjusters, and private insurance adjusters.

d) the Moped- cute, efficient, and quiet means of transportation - something many motorcyclists wouldn't dare be seen on.

the Land Yacht, a fully dressed touring bike

N

Names

– cars are not called the 'Geek' or the 'Zit' for very good reason - the name of a car is its crowning glory, and to have anything but the most inspiring moniker hung from its fender would doom a car to cruddy sales. Manufacturers have narrowed down potential names by eliminating whole classes of *verboten* sources, the 3 worst being: 1/ Diseases, 2/ Wimpy Animals, and 3/ Bodily Functions. Among those left up to corporate discretion are Famous Places (the Camargue is a 'go' whereas the Bronx is not) and Star Constellations ('yes' to Taurus the Bull, 'no' to Petey the Busboy).

Rumour has it that at least one major company is dabbling in Foods right now. Industry insiders claim they've zeroed in on Cereals and Grains, but may look to Vegetables if they don't come up with anything more exciting than 'Bulgur'.

Neutral

– state of gear disengagement in a transmission. However, to say aloud, "That chap's gears are disengaged!" would be an automotive insult slung at other drivers in lieu of more banal references to cheese slipping off crackers, or dancing with the music off.

Night

– dark time of day, when pedestrians, bushes, other traffic, the road, and buildings are indistinguishable.

clip and save special!

If where you're driving ever looks like this — back up quick

No
- frequent response to young drivers asking to borrow the car.

Nuts
- dense objects found either holding parts of the car together, or doing something foolish behind the steering wheel.

Off-Road Recovery
- emergency corrective action taken when a vehicle wanders onto gravel shoulders. To avoid high-speed disaster, a controlled and cautious arm swing at the steering wheel is needed to cut sharply back to the highway once speed is reduced. Breathing and pulse rate can later be recovered off-road through repeated, less cautious arm swings of a choice beverage.

One-Way Street
- single direction roadway 2nd only to prune juice at speeding up movement by relieving congested blocks.

Ornament

– useless, gaudy looking addition to any vehicle. Many types of ornaments, including the classic 'dangling fuzzy dice', may be picked up at auto parts shops for a couple of bucks. Other kinds - the most favoured being of the giggly, blonde-haired variety - can be picked up at many bars for a couple of drinks.

Overpass

– shooting right by a slower vehicle and winding up in a field.

Parking

– just like simultaneously patting your head while rubbing your stomach, parking a vehicle requires an orchestration of dexterities that can bring grown men to tears. Extra difficulty ensues when:
    a) you're driving a van with no mirrors.
    b) you've got dogs or pre-school children along for the ride.
    c) the owner(s) of the car(s) parked ahead of and/or behind your space is/are there to watch you.

Passenger

– versatile talking seatcover that can double as a map-reading, cassette-flipping grocery–carrier.

Parking (Checklist)

DOWNHILL:
- Wheels turned to the right
- Engine in gear
- Parking brake on

UPHILL:
- Wheels turned to the left
- Engine in gear
- Parking brake on

ANY HILL,
CAR'S A LEMON:
- Insurance policy in order
- Wheels straight ahead
- Engine in neutral
- Parking brake off

Q

Quagmire

– swampy soup of mud, snow or sand, in which a car can become stuck. A technique known as 'rocking' (quickly shifting the transmission between forward and reverse to set up a rhythm) can often free a car by creating a sight so pathetic that passersby will be compelled to help push.

R

R & R

– service garage shorthand for 'remove and replace' - referring to the practice of no longer repairing a worn-out part, but instead replacing it with another to save time and money. This expedient solution can still cost megabucks, and it's no wonder that alternatives like D & D (drive and disregard) and the simple R (remove) are catching on.

Race

– contest of speed requiring precision, cunning, and finely honed reflexes. Hold on either a special course for vast financial reward or in a parking lot for the last remaining space.

Radar

– (fam.) speed detection device. As a service to all traffic police reading this book, it should be mentioned that recent studies suggest a connection between the use of radar equipment, and impotence.

Radials

– 2nd most popular targets of car thieves.

Ragtop

Radios

– most popular targets of car thieves.

Ragtop

– 1/ man with a toupee driving a 2/ convertible.

Reaction

– behaviour triggered by stimulus. In driving, this is often measured as Distance Travelled; for instance, the span between when a driver perceives a threat (stimulus), and when the driver begins to respond to it - this frequently being equal to the stretch covered between when a threat is responded to, and when it's hit.

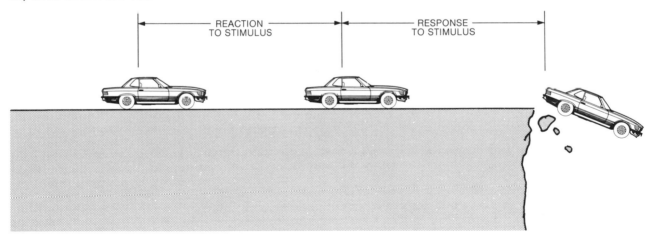

REACTION
TO STIMULUS

RESPONSE
TO STIMULUS

Red
– colour of expensive, flashy, sports cars most likely to turn other drivers green with envy.

Reverse
– alternate direction in which to scrape fenders, bang bumpers and run over things.

Retread
– 1/ outdated practice of covering a worn-out tire with a new rubber tread.
2/ person who still believes this to be a great idea.

Right-of-Way
– guideline for yielding to other drivers. For those less inclined to social graces, there's also the Okay-of-Way. In essence, this is the Right-of-Way with loopholes permitting selfish acts brought on by a) driving in a strange town, b) poor brakes, or c) being late.

The Wrong-of-Way covers maniacs and pinheads. This allows for demented behaviour caused by anything from needing a tune-up to having been dropped during infancy.

Road Hog

– selfish driver. Blocks others due to a lack of both consideration and alertness. Though the urge to ram a hog up his or her bacon may be hard to resist, try to channel your frustrations into more socially acceptable outlets . . . like reverse-written signs

BRIGHT MOVE, CAT BREATH! or GUN IT, YOU SWINE

for hogs *using* their mirrors - an unlikely hope at the best of times. If this diplomatic approach to reform doesn't improve the hogs' driving . . . then by all means ram them up their bacon.

Rush Hour

– time of day when any kind of rush trip will take at least an hour.

S

Saint Christopher

– patron saint of travellers. Legend has it that Saint Christopher was a giant who one day carried a child over a river and said, "Chylde, thou hast put me in great peryll. I might bere no greater burden." The child answered, "Marvel thou nothing, for thou hast borne all the world upon thee, and its sins likewise." Popular opinion claims this to be an allegory of Christ the child being carried over the River of Death. Noted historian, Jacob Rott, claims that the child spoke further, " . . . and next tyme, why not tryeth the footbrydge over yon?", to which Saint Christopher responded, "I thryveth on perylls, kyd, don't cramp my style."

Currently a campaign is underway through the Unified Drive-In Church and Gospel Co-op to sell Saint Christopher blessings by cassette. For 10% of a driver's annual wages, the church guarantees travel safety - excepting accidents caused by carelessness and Acts of God. Their special "Half-Holy Mini-Package" is tailored to the budget-minded. For 5% of his or her income, a driver is assured of choice parking spots in most major cities.

Salesman

- only obstacle between you and your dream car. Until car buying is self-serve, us drivers are obliged to endure the salesman's inevitable monologue, and woe be it to the potential buyer unable to interpret Salespeak - the language of these showroom birds of prey. As a rule, never trust anything said containing these words or phrases:

- *I would myself*
- *the quietest yet*
- *they're genuine*
- *the best*
- *guaranteed*
- *definitely*

- *economical*
- *very*
- *super*
- *never*
- *always*
- *yes*
- *no*

Screw-Up
- any driving manoeuvre that creates more hazard than it's worth.

Seat Belts
- the dental floss of driving . . . not a thrill to use, but undeniably helpful.

Self-Serve Station
- one of the most frustrating necessities of driving, as shown in this poem from *Driver's Almanac*:

There once was a man from Duluth,
who, when sworn to telling the truth,
said, "I wouldn't pay,
for gas gotten that day
from the pump that was third from the booth."

In tears of frustration, arrested,
he yelled, he cried, he confessed it:
" . . . got the gun from my trunk,
and then shot the pump,
to get the nozzle shut off when I wanted."

Sense of Humour
- 1/ being able to kid someone about their poor driving habits.
- 2/ not belting someone kidding you about your poor driving habits.

Shock Absorbers
- 1/ gas-filled, suspension-dampening devices.
- 2/ credit cards used to pay for the replacement of 1/.

Skill
- what most drivers think their Screw-Up showed.

Seat Belts *(the Scene Behind the Scene)*

UNBELTED DUMMY

BELTED DUMMY

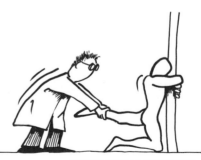

SMART DUMMY

Spare

Slush
- chilly, semi-liquid street snow found in bottomless puddles at the edges of roads. Has corrosive effect on vehicles.

Splash
- dramatic event occurring when slush is driven through. Has corrosive effect on nearby pedestrians.

Spare
- (*fam.*) extra tire and wheel assembly carried in a vehicle's trunk, that was last seen two summers ago and now has no more than 3 p.s.i. of air in it.

Speed
- sort of like sleep - the wrong amount can create problems. Mind you, the police are more apt to stop you for having too much speed than too much sleep. Unless you're sleeping and speeding at the same time, in which case you'll wish you were home in bed.

Stereo
- 1/ favourite accessory of music lovers.
  2/ frightening accessory for anyone when left switched on at its previous volume in a car that's just being started.

Swerve
- driving tactic used to avoid hitting Ugly Stuff (*see* **Ugly Stuff**).

T

Tailgating
- driving extremely close behind a slower vehicle. Studies have shown that while this dangerous practice fails to make the 1st car speed up, it significantly cuts down on bugs in the 2nd car's grill.

Tank
- nickname given simultaneously to large, gaudy cars and the large, gaudy people driving them.

Theft
- thrilling and inexpensive way to 'trade up'.

Ticket
- bill given by police to drivers committing infractions - prized for its absorbency when wiping dipsticks during oil checks.

Tailgating (Compulsive Behaviour in Some)

Toll Booths
– government-generated highway cow pies.

Traffic Jam
– sort of a motorized purgatory. Frequently caused by accidents, mouth-breathing rubberneckers slowing to look at accidents, and those ineptly-named times of day known as Rush Hour. When drivers are tailgating or not looking far enough ahead, we often get the 'domino effect' jam: one driver's brakelights trigger an avalanche of over–reaction that culminates in poor saps at the end having to come to a complete halt.

Psychologists at Our Mother of Merging Hospital have come up with a suggestion of why so many people pick their noses when caught in a traffic jam. Seemingly, the Reaming Reflex as they called it, stems back to childhood - a time when comfort is sought through nose-picking and sucking thumbs. As with kids, drivers are not immune to wanting a digit up their nostril when they too are alone in a crowd, tired, cranky and want to go home. When firmly anchored in your next traffic jam, try to make a game of it. Count the number of nose-pickers you see, and score things this way:

> 1 point - each nose-picker
> 2 points - each nose-picker who spots you watching
> * bonus point - if you don't break out laughing

Trucks

– highly contagious highway disease. You'll know you have 'trucks' when you glance in your mirror and see something like:

The cure almost always involves accelerating well over the speed limit, in which case you'll then become susceptible to another dangerous ailment known as 'cops'.

Trust

– da ting dat pushes ya back in yer seat when ya hit da gas.

Turbo

– Most Desirable Gadget of the Decade. A small device which simultaneously compresses the incoming fuel mixture to the engine while sucking outgoing car payments from the wallet.

U

U-Turn
– just for kicks, take your hands off the steering wheel and yell this to your passenger.

Ugly Stuff
– any noun in a driver's path.

V

Vanguard
– 1/ quaint English sedan of the '60's.
2/ chained-up killer English pit bull terrier.

Villain
– see **Insurance Broker**.

Visors
– adjustable flaps that swing down to almost block out a rising/setting sun.

W

Wagons

– *Historical:* commonly seen parked in circles for security, as large pioneer families moved westward to the mountains.

Modern Day: commonly seen parked in lots for shopping, as large middle-class families move outward to the suburbs.

Wash and Wax

– modern day rain dance, usually performed on Saturdays. In trying to explain why it so often rains on cars that have been polished for three hours, experts have suggested that the hand and body motions of car owners closely resemble those of ancient tribal rituals used to please the rain gods. Relics found that depict Aztec floor mat vacuumings and ash tray dumpings support this theory.

Wash and Wax

Wet Leaves

- practical joke Mother Nature plays on motorcyclists every Autumn.

Winter

- the first moments of a winter snowfall are good times to test your car's handling and traction. Key points to remember:

1/ Practise spins and slides in wide-open parking lots. This cuts down on pant-wetting close calls by teaching you things about control that are too dangerous to learn on the streets.

2/ Snow banks can be your friends. If you find yourself going too fast, you can often scrub off lots of speed by kissing a curbside pile of snow at the proper angle. At improper angle would be one that scrubs off all of your speed, and requires a tow-truck to get you going again.

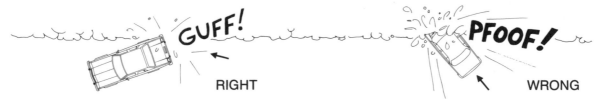

Winter Survival

- the car's gone pud. You're stranded. A blizzard is blizzing, and not a soul is in sight. Your options: commence wailing and gnashing of teeth, or else break out the following:

1/ Granola Bars - edible sticks of birdseed, glue and woodchips which can almost be appealing in a crisis. If not, they can serve as crucial traction aids when unwrapped and chucked under drive wheels.

2/ Blanket - provider of essential warmth. In extremely cold situations it can be stuffed under the gas tank as kindling for a car blaze, while in relatively mild conditions it can be spread on the snow for an ant-free picnic.

3/ Shovel - spade-like device for digging out of snow drifts and fighting off small to mid-size animals.

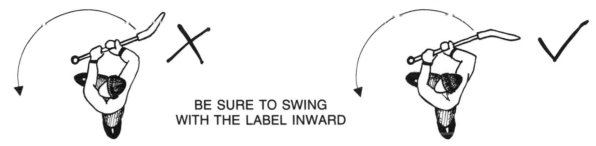

BE SURE TO SWING WITH THE LABEL INWARD

4/ Can Opener - entertaining prop for "Dashboard Hallucination Theatre" - a form of amusement often initiated by drivers suffering acute head frostbite.

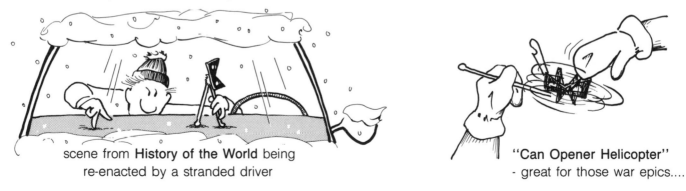

scene from **History of the World** being re-enacted by a stranded driver

"Can Opener Helicopter" - great for those war epics....

5/ Candles - flammable sticks of wax, used when food supply dwindles. Take only small bites, and be sure to chew well. Save those wicks, too. In a pinch, they can double for dental floss, clothesline, etc.

6/ Diary - daily log of events. Who knows - besides keeping the mind sharp, it could later on form the basis of a movie.

7/ Flashlight - for nighttime diversions like "Spot the Wolf" and "Blind the Bear".

X

X
- one of the two requisite buzzletters to have in a hot-selling sports car's name.

Y

Yammer
- distracting chat between driver and passengers.

Yikes
- exclamation of yammering driver on looking forward at the traffic stopped too close ahead.

Yonder

Yonder
- fabled destination reckoned by locals to be the place you're asking directions to when lost on holidays.

Z

Z
- the other requisite buzzletter to have in a hot-selling sports car's name.

Zerk
- name for the delicate grease fitting found on many chassis points requiring lubrication.

Zerk!
- sound heard by weekend mechanic as an over-tightened zerk fitting snaps in two.

ABOUT THE AUTHOR/CARTOONIST

In pursuing a career as a race car driver, Stephen Barnes found himself with more skill than money; the high-profile living sapped his funds, leaving him destitute. The villa in Monaco had to go. The friends and admirers, the champagne celebrations .... all of it .... *Pfffft*!

For the next two years, the chump even had to ride the bus, though he kept insisting this was temporary as his car was in for service. How pathetic. Just as things hit rock bottom, he awoke one morning on the park bench and noticed an ad on his newspaper blanket - "Writers/Cartoonists needed. Some heavy lifting required." In desperation he took the job, unaware that the demand for hand-lettered supermarket produce signs was about to skyrocket. In no time at all he was crawling out of debt, piecing his life together again.

Now the fool wants another shot at driving race cars.

Would you buy a book from this man?